A Note to Parents

DK READERS is a compelling program for beginning readers, designed in conjunction with leading literacy experts, including Dr. Linda Gambrell, Professor of Education at Clemson University. Dr. Gambrell has served as President of the National Reading Conference, the College Reading Association, and the International Reading Association.

The DK ReaderActives line provides action-oriented illustrations, colorful page designs, and stories in which children get to make their own choices. Multiple story paths encourage children to reread their adventures to explore every possible ending. Each DK ReaderActive is guaranteed to capture a child's interest while developing his or her reading skills, general knowledge, and love of reading.

Unlike DK READERS, DK ReaderActives are not assigned a specific reading level. Generally, DK ReaderActives are best suited to Levels 2 and 3 in the list below. Younger children will surely enjoy making the story's choices while adults read aloud to them. Likewise, older children will appreciate picking their own path and trying new options with each reading.

Pre-level 1: Learning to read
Level 1: Beginning to read
Level 2: Beginning to read alone
Level 3: Reading alone
Level 4: Proficient readers

The "normal" age at which a child begins to read can be anywhere from three to eight years old. Adult participation through the lower levels is very helpful for providing encouragement, discussing storylines, and sounding out unfamiliar words. No matter which ReaderActive title you select, you can be sure that you are helping your child learn to read interactively!

DK

LONDON, NEW YORK, MUNICH,
MELBOURNE, AND DELHI

For DK/BradyGames

Global Strategy Guide Publisher
Mike Degler

Licensing Manager
Christian Sumner

Editor-In-Chief
H. Leigh Davis

Operations Manager
Stacey Beheler

Title Manager
Tim Fitzpatrick

Book Designer
Tim Amrhein

Production Designer
Wil Cruz

Reading Consultant
Linda B. Gambrell, Ph.D.

© 2012 DK/BradyGAMES, a division of Penguin Group (USA) Inc.
BradyGames® is a registered trademark of Penguin Group (USA)
Inc. All rights reserved, including the right of reproduction in whole
or in part in any form.

© 2012 Pokémon. © 1995–2012 Nintendo/Creatures Inc./
GAME FREAK inc. TM, ®, and character names are
trademarks of Nintendo.

DK/BradyGAMES
800 East 96th St., 3rd floor
Indianapolis, IN 46240

12 13 14   10 9 8 7 6 5 4 3 2 1

A catalog record for this book is available from the Library of Congress.

ISBN: 978-0-7566-5375-0 (Paperback)

Printed and bound by Lake Book Manufacturing, Inc.

Discover more at

www.dk.com

Your First Pokémon!

Written by Simcha Whitehill

DK Publishing

HOW TO USE THIS READERACTIVE

Welcome to this Pokémon ReaderActive, where *you* decide how the story unfolds! As you read, you'll find instructions at the bottom of each section of the story. These instructions fall into three categories:

1. Some instructions tell you to skip to a certain page—they look like this:

> Continue to **PAGE 31** and choose your first Pokémon!

When you see an instruction like this, simply turn to the page that's listed and continue reading.

2. Other instructions let you make a choice. This is how you decide where the story takes you! Each of your options is described in its own bar, like this:

> If you want Oshawott to make a big blast and ride the wave out, go to **PAGE 10**, **BOTTOM**.

> If you want Oshawott to fill the hole gently like a pool and swim its way out, go to **PAGE 42**.

Whichever option you choose, just skip to the listed page and continue reading. In the example above, let's say you decide to choose the first option. In that case, just turn to **PAGE 10**. Notice that the instruction also tells you to read the **BOTTOM** entry. Sometimes instructions tell you to read the **TOP** or the **BOTTOM** of a certain page. Pay attention to this—when you turn to such a page, you'll see that the entries are marked with the words "TOP" and "BOTTOM," like this:

Just be sure to read the right entry for your choice!

3. Every now and then, you'll reach a part of the story that is decided by chance. This is called a "Challenge." Most of the time, you'll flip a coin to determine the outcome. Here's what a Challenge section looks like:

Flip a coin and use the results to determine your path.

(H) **HEADS**
If you land on heads, head to **PAGE 55**, **TOP**.

(T) **TAILS**
For tails, proceed to **PAGE 63**.

Depending on whether you get "heads" or "tails," simply turn to the indicated page and resume reading. In the example above, let's say you flip a coin and get "tails." In that case, turn to **PAGE 63** and continue the story.

That's all there is to it! Don't forget—when you finish one story, you can start over, make different choices, and create a whole new adventure! Now it's time to choose your first Pokémon—have fun!

WELCOME TO PROFESSOR JUNIPER'S LAB!

You have just arrived in Nuvema Town to start your adventure as a Pokémon Trainer! Professor Juniper leads you through her lab to a very special room. There, Unova's three starter Pokémon await you: Tepig, Snivy, and Oshawott.

"Which one you choose is entirely up to you," Professor Juniper says, handing you a Pokédex.

Before you decide, you use your Pokédex to learn a little about each one.

Continue to **PAGE 31** and choose your first Pokémon!

Snivy picks a sunny spot next to the web to suntan. It's trying to trick Galvantula into thinking that it's easy prey. Galvantula falls for the trap and crawls off the web to come snag Snivy. However, super smart Snivy actually uses the sunshine to power up so it can speed away.

"Sniiiiiiivvvvvvvvyyyyyy!" it says, as it disappears into the woods.

Before Galvantula can get back on the web, you quickly set Minccino free. Now, Galvantula crawls straight for you, and it is mad!

"Galvantulaaaaaaaa!" it yells.

To run, go to **PAGE 34**.

To wait for Snivy to come back to battle Galvantula, go to **PAGE 39**.

Swadloon's Trainer comes running from picking berries in the woods.

"Are you okay, Swadloon?" the tall Trainer asks.

You tell him that it was an accident and apologize for Tepig's stray Ember attack hitting Swadloon.

"These things happen. No worries! I'm Fitzy, by the way," he says. "Hey, do you and Tepig want to use that fiery spunk in a practice battle against me and Swadloon?"

"Of course! Right, Tepig?" you cheer.

"Tepig!" it agrees.

Proceed to **PAGE 9, BOTTOM**.

Now, you have a chance to catch your first Pokémon: Minccino! However, you and Snivy must first battle it.

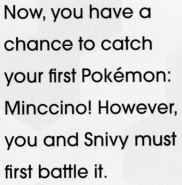

Two different attacks come to mind as you and Snivy prepare to battle Minccino: Leech Seed and Vine Whip. Now is the time to tell Snivy which one to use.

To have Snivy start with Leech Seed, proceed to **PAGE 50**.

To use Vine Whip, go to **PAGE 24**.

Too late! Swadloon ties up Tepig in String Shot.

You shout, "Quick, Tepig, use Ember to burn it off!"

Tepig breaks free with fire, but now, it is also weaker. What move should Tepig use next?

To have Tepig use Defense Curl, go to **PAGE 54**.

To have Tepig get close to Swadloon with Tackle, go to **PAGE 40**, **TOP**.

Your first battle with Tepig is on!

"Okay, use Tackle!" you say.

Tepig races across the field, but Swadloon dodges the move.

"Nice one, Swadloon! Now, use Razor Leaf," Fitzy instructs.

What do you think Tepig should do now?

To have Tepig use Defense Curl to shield itself from Razor Leaf, proceed to **PAGE 51**.

To have Tepig fire back with Ember, proceed to **PAGE 26**.

I Choose You, Snivy!

As you and Snivy are walking through the woods, you spot Minccino caught in Galvantula's web. Both you and Snivy want to help the tied up Normal-type, but how? Galvantula is standing guard at its web!

If you want Snivy to use Leaf Tornado to scare off Galvantula, go to **PAGE 56**.

To come up with a plan to distract Galvantula, go to **PAGE 6**.

BOTTOM

"Oshaaaaaa!" it yelps, blasting Water Gun. Oshawott flies out of the hole. "You did it!" you cheer.

Then suddenly, you hear Drilbur, and it's headed this way! Oshawott's Water Gun attack has left Drilbur's hole in a terrible state. Do you stick around to help Drilbur, or do you make a break for it?

To run for it, go to **PAGE 60, TOP**.

To say hello to Drilbur, continue to **PAGE 37**.

You know that there must be a way for Oshawott to rescue itself with Water Gun.

"Are you with me, pal?" you ask Oshawott.

"Osha!" it nods.

Now it's just
a matter
of how
to use
the attack…

If you want Oshawott to make a big blast
and ride the wave out, go to **PAGE 10**, **BOTTOM**.

If you want Oshawott to fill the hole gently like a pool
and swim its way out, go to **PAGE 42**.

Congratulations! You have caught your first wild Pokémon—a super cool Swadloon!

"Thank you, Tepig. I couldn't have done it without you, buddy," you say.

It nuzzles you and cheers, "Tepig!"

With one victory, you have made two new Pokémon friends.

THE END

"Snivy!" you shout, hoping it will hear your call.

In the meantime, Minccino decides to do some screaming of its own. "Minccinoooooooooooooooh!" it yelps, unleashing Hyper Voice.

In one loud and powerful move, Minccino scares off Galvantula and signals your location to Snivy. "Snivy!" it announces, upon its return.

Now that you're back together, you have one thing on your mind: catching your new friend Minccino.

It's time to take the **Change Challenge**!

Flip a coin and use the results to determine your path.

 HEADS
If you land on heads, go to **PAGE 49**.

 TAILS
If you land on tails, go to **PAGE 58**.

"Stop it! You're so embarrassing," you yell.

Tepig snarls back at you.

Nurse Joy chimes in, "You both need to learn to treat each other with respect."

She asks Audino to use the feelers on its ears to sense how Tepig feels. With Audino's help and some common-sense reasoning, you figure out that Tepig is upset. It is homesick and misses Professor Juniper's lab.

Wanting to be an understanding Trainer, you say, "I know how you feel. I just left my home to become a Trainer." You continue, "So, I promise to be there for you!"

Tepig smiles knowing that it has a friend in you.

"Now, how about we start out on a big adventure together?" you ask.

"Tepig!" it cheers.

THE END

You decide you can't keep running from Galvantula. So, you turn around and stand your ground. Minccino is inspired by your bravery. It decides to stop and stand by you as well.

"Galvvvvv," Galvantula snarls.

"Minccino!" it announces it's now in battle mode. Then, it unleashes a Double Slap.

All of a sudden, Snivy swoops onto the scene. It ties up Galvantula with Vine Whip.

"Glad you found us, buddy!" you say to Snivy.

Minccino uses Tickle. Then, Snivy finishes the battle with Wrap.

You cheer, "Way to go team!"

And that's when it hits you—you have to try to catch Minccino! You quickly throw a Poké Ball and catch your new Pokémon pal.

"I couldn't have done it without you, Snivy," you say.

"Snivy!" it replies, happy to have not just one, but two new friends.

THE END

You explain what happened to Drilbur and say that you're sorry. You promise, "We'll help you dig a new hole."

"Osha, osha!" your Water-type Pokémon says, scooping up dirt with its scalchop. Drilbur accepts your apology. Together, you all pitch in and dig out a new hole.

"All right, we did it!" you say.

"Drilbur dril!" the wild, digging Pokémon says with a smile.

You suggest a battle with your powerful Pokémon friend, Drilbur.

"Drilbur!" it says, ready to go.

Continue to **PAGE 21**.

"Drilllllll!" it says, digging a diagonal path down to the bottom of the hole.

It clears a way for Oshawott to walk up and out.

You cheer Drilbur's effort, "Hooray!"

You and Oshawott thank Drilbur for coming to the rescue. Then, you ask it if it would like to be the first Pokémon that you and Oshawott battle.

"Drilbur!" it says, ready to have some fun.

If you want Oshawott to kick off the battle with Tail Whip, go to **PAGE 30**.

If you want to let Drilbur make the first move, go to **PAGE 38**.

Like a good sport, you thank Fitzy for the awesome battle.

"Looking forward to a rematch!" he replies, shaking your hand.

You and Tepig return to the road.

As you walk away, you say, "Tepig, you were amazing out there in your first battle! I know that if we work hard, we'll be a great team!"

"Tepig!" it agrees, smiling.

After a rough start to the day, you're happy you chose Tepig.

THE END

It's a busy day at the Pokémon Center. There's a long line to see Nurse Joy. Tepig does not like to wait, so it snorts fire. This may lead to trouble if Tepig accidentally hits somebody.

Taking Tepig outside might be a wise choice to make sure it doesn't cause any problems. However, doing so would mean losing your place in line.

If you decide to take Tepig outside because you're worried it might cause problems, go to **PAGE 59**.

If you stay indoors because you don't want to lose your place in line, go to **PAGE 40**, **BOTTOM**.

"Thanks," you say to Xian, "but today is the first day that Snivy and I have traveled together. We want to get back on the road."

Xian replies, "Well, I hope we run into each other again someday."

As you shake Xian's hand, you add, "When we do, the battle will be on!"

Your Grass-type Pokémon companion cheers, "Snivy!"

THE END

Oshawott strikes first with a wet and wild Water Pulse. Drilbur tries to respond with Scratch, but Oshawott blocks it with Water Gun. The powerful counterattack knocks Drilbur off its feet. You quickly throw your Poké Ball and catch your new pal, Drilbur.

"All right, it's official! Now, we'll all be best friends forever," you say.

"Osha!" it cheers.

THE END

You see Drilbur coming up the path. Perfect timing—you bet it can help!

You ask, "Can you please help Oshawott?"

"Drilbur!" it says. It's happy to do what it can.

It's time to suggest a way for Drilbur to assist Oshawott. How should Drilbur rescue your Water-type Pokémon pal?

To have Drilbur dig a path out, go to **PAGE 17**.

To have Drilbur jump into the hole so it can hoist up Oshawott, go to **PAGE 45**.

Luckily, Nurse Joy gives Snivy a potion that brings it back to normal in no time. Tepig shows that it's sorry.

You add to Tepig's apology, confessing, "I'm sorry too. Tepig and I have had a hard first day."

Always helpful, Nurse Joy brings in an Audino. She tells it to use the special feelers on its ears to sense how Tepig is feeling.

"Audino," it sighs, hinting that Tepig is upset.

It's clear that you and Tepig need to have a good talk. Tepig seems nervous about making a new friend. You have shown Tepig that you'll stand by it, even when it makes a mistake—like hitting Snivy with Ember.

"I will always be here for you, buddy!" you assure Tepig with a hug.

Audino is happy to see you two make up and cheers, "Audino!"

Now, you and Tepig are ready to continue your adventure together as a team!

THE END

Snivy grabs Minccino with Vine Whip. While Snivy has it tied, you quickly throw a Poké Ball.

"All right! I caught my first Pokémon!" you cheer.

"Snivy!" it adds, sharing your excitement.

Hugging your friend, you say, "Of course, buddy; I owe you a big thanks! I couldn't have done it without you."

"Snivy!" it says, smiling.

In one day as a Pokémon Trainer, you have made two very special friends.

THE END

You hear a strange noise in the bushes. Galvantula might be out of the way, but it sounds like something else is headed straight for you. What could it be?

Galvantula is gone, but Minccino is still in Galvantula's web. Is it safe to explore the source of the noise, or would you rather try to catch Minccino?

To ignore the noise and focus on Minccino, go to **PAGE 55, BOTTOM**.

To investigate the source of the mysterious noise, go to **PAGE 41**.

Tepig snorts a fiery Ember.

You yell, "Quick Tepig, add Flame Charge!"

Tepig looks like a ball of fire as it races across the battlefield toward Swadloon. Landing a hit with a huge blast, Tepig wins its first match.

"Way to go, Tepig!" you cheer. Then, like a good sport, you thank Fitzy for the great battle.

"Congratulations!" Fitzy says, "You two are already an awesome team. I hope our paths will cross again and we get to have a rematch."

"Looking forward to it," you say. "Until next time…"

THE END

Galvantula crawls up close because it wants to sink its chompers into Snivy with Bug Bite. However, Snivy stops it in its tracks with a serious stare of Leer.

"Sniiiiiivy!" it shouts, blowing it away in Leaf Tornado.

Next, Snivy wraps it up in Vine Whip.

"Galvantula!" the opponent yells, caught in Snivy's trap.

Then, Snivy uses a strong squeeze of Wrap to win the battle.

You exclaim, "All right, Snivy! You did it!"

Continue to **PAGE 8**.

To help Tepig feel more comfortable expressing its feelings, you say, "I know we're new friends, Tepig, but whatever it is, you can tell me."

And just like that, Tepig's eyes get teary and its angry fire stops. Tepig realizes that you really care about it. It nuzzles your leg with its nose.

"Aw, shucks, Tepig! I am always here to listen. That's what friends are for!" you say, petting it.

And now it looks like you two are going to be best buddies!

"So, what do you say we put that Ember to good use and start practicing?" you ask.

"Tepig!" it says, raring to go.

THE END

Congratulations! Minccino is your new Pokémon pal.

You cheer, "Hooray! I couldn't have done it without you, Snivy. To top it all off, it was our first battle!"

"Snivy!" it says, with a smile.

After such a long day, you put Snivy back in its Poké Ball so it can get a good rest. You start back out on the path, excited for all the adventures that await you and your new Pokémon pals, Snivy and Minccino.

THE END

"Osha!" the Water-type shouts, wagging Tail Whip to distract Drilbur and lower its defenses.

Drilbur responds by chucking Rock Slide.

You tell Oshawott, "Use your scalchop to block the boulders!"

However, the scalchop gets knocked out of its hand. Now, Drilbur gets up close to deliver a double blow: dishing dirt with Mud-Slap and scratching Fury Swipes.

"Osha!" it sighs. Drilbur wins the round.

"Thank you so much for the battle," you say. Drilbur nods and wanders back into the woods.

You encourage your friend, "You were great out there in your first battle, Oshawott! With practice, we'll just get better and better."

"Osha!" it agrees.

THE END

Snivy: The Grass Snake Pokémon

Calm and intelligent, Snivy speeds up when exposed to large amounts of sunlight. By bathing its tail in sunlight, it can photosynthesize. But if it feels unwell, its tail droops.

TYPE	Grass
HEIGHT	2'00"
WEIGHT	17.9 lbs.

Tepig: The Fire Pig Pokémon

TYPE	Fire
HEIGHT	1'08"
WEIGHT	21.8 lbs.

Tepig can blow fire from its nose, whether to launch fireballs at an opponent or roast berries for food. But if it catches a cold, it blows out black smoke instead of flames.

Oshawott: The Sea Otter Pokémon

The detachable scalchop on Oshawott's stomach is made from the same material as claws. Oshawott uses the scalchop like a blade, and will slash at an attacking foe.

TYPE	Water
HEIGHT	1'08"
WEIGHT	13.0 lbs.

If you want to choose SNIVY, go to **PAGE 10**, **TOP**.

If you want to choose TEPIG, go to **PAGE 43**.

If you want to choose OSHAWOTT, go to **PAGE 33**.

You arrive at a fork in the road. You want to go left but Tepig wants to go right. To get its way, Tepig snorts fire at a bush—but that bush is actually a Swadloon!

"Swadloooooon!" it yells.

Uh oh, it looks like Tepig has just picked a fight.

Suddenly, you hear noises in the distance that sound like they're getting closer.

If you want to figure out what the noise is, proceed to **PAGE 7**.

If you want to deal with Swadloon first, go to **PAGE 35, BOTTOM**.

I Choose You, Oshawott!

You're so excited and nervous to have a new friend that you can't stop talking. In fact, you're so busy rambling that it takes you a while to realize Oshawott isn't even there! Where could it possibly be?

"Oh no!" you shout.

You hear a faint cry in the distance. You run toward it and find Oshawott. It fell into a deep hole. Based on the claw-like markings, you think it was probably dug by a wild Drilbur.

You reassure Oshawott, "Don't worry, buddy. I'm going to get you out of there!"

How can you rescue it from the hole?

To grab a rope, go to **PAGE 46**.

To have Oshawott use a Water-type move and swim out, go to **PAGE 11**.

To wait for help, proceed **PAGE 22**.

"Run!" you tell Minccino.

You both try to make a break for the woods. Galvantula is right behind you. You have to make your move—and soon!

You might still be able to outrun Galvantula. On the other hand, maybe stopping to battle is smart.

To take your chances and keep running, go to **PAGE 13**.

To stop and see if Minccino will help you battle back Galvantula, go to **PAGE 15**.

Oh no! When you left Tepig to grab Nurse Joy for help, it picked a fight with another Trainer's Pansage. Tepig hit the Grass-type with an angry Ember attack.

"Tepig, stop!" you scream, trying to break up the commotion.

It's time to take the **Change Challenge**!

Flip a coin and use the results to determine your path.

 HEADS
If you land on heads, head to **PAGE 55, TOP**.

 TAILS
For tails, proceed to **PAGE 63**.

You think to yourself, "Maybe I can get Tepig to apologize to Swadloon to avoid a fight."

To find out, you need to take the

Change Challenge!

Flip a coin and use the results to determine your path.

 HEADS
If you land on heads, head to **PAGE 57**.

 TAILS
For tails, proceed to **PAGE 9, TOP**.

You quickly snag Minccino from Galvantula's web, and not a moment too soon. Galvantula has snapped out of its dizzy spell from Leaf Tornado; now it's ready to battle you!

"Galvantulaaaaaa!" it says, using Thunder Wave to spray electricity everywhere.

You whisper, "Let's scatter so Galvantula won't know who to chase."

You and Snivy run one way, while Minccino runs the other. Galvantula chases after you. However, you two are too fast, even for its six legs! After helping Minccino escape, you're confident that you and Snivy are ready to take on any challenge that comes your way!

THE END

When Drilbur sees that its hole is ruined, it screams, "Drilllllburrrrrr!"

"Uh oh," you whisper to Oshawott.

Drilbur is so mad that it nearly knocks over you and Oshawott with Earthquake. Since you and Oshawott made the mess, you can try to patch things up with Drilbur, or you can turn the tables and battle it.

To try to smooth things over by saying you're sorry, go to **PAGE 16**.

To have Oshawott fight back with Water Pulse, go to **PAGE 21**.

Drilbur gets down into the ground with Dig. However, the surprise is on Drilbur, because Oshawott dodges it. Then, Oshawott fires a blast of Water Gun and adds swipes of Razor Shell.

"Osha, osha, osha!" it says, swinging its scalchop.

Drilbur is unable to battle.

"Way to go Oshawott!" you cheer.

Then, you act fast and toss a Poké Ball.

"Fingers crossed," you whisper, hoping to catch the Mole Pokémon.

Congratulations! You are now the proud Trainer of one very cool Drilbur too.

"Osha!" the Water-type cheers for its new friend.

"Snivy!" it announces—it's back.

Galvantula shoots a sticky String Shot, but super slick Snivy dodges it.

"Use Tackle!" you suggest.

However, just as Snivy gets close to Galvantula, the creepy crawly scratches it with Fury Cutter.
This battle is a tough one!

If you think Snivy can handle it all on its own, go to **PAGE 27**.

To call on Minccino to help, go to **PAGE 52**.

TOP

Tepig charges forward with Tackle. Just as it's about to hit Swadloon, you tell it to add a blast of fiery Ember. These two moves deliver a real double whammy!

"Awesome, Tepig! Keep firing Ember," you add.

Caught in a shower of sparks, Grass-type Swadloon is worn down. Tepig wins the round. You quickly grab a Poké Ball and toss it straight at Swadloon.

Proceed to **PAGE 12** to see if you catch it.

BOTTOM

Tepig is out of control! It's running wild around the Pokémon Center lobby, and it refuses to wait in line with you.

You plead, "Come on, Tepig—get back here!"

Everyone is staring at you. You have to do something, and fast!

If you want to grab Nurse Joy for help, go to **PAGE 35**, **TOP**.

If you want to take Tepig out of the lobby, and fast, proceed to **PAGE 48**.

As you help Minccino down from the web, a boy runs toward the scene. It's Minccino's Trainer.

Happy to see its pal, the rescued Pokémon exclaims, "Minccino!"

"Hi, I'm Xian. Nice to meet ya!" he says, introducing himself.

Xian tells you that he and Minccino went for a walk while his other Pokémon, Axew, rested at the Pokémon Center. So, when Galvantula jumped out and grabbed Minccino, Xian couldn't stop it alone. He ran to get help, but luckily you and Snivy came along.

Xian adds, "I just can't thank you enough!"

"Snivy and I were happy to help," you reply.

Eager to get some practice, you ask Xian if he would like to battle.

Xian replies, "Sure! First, though, I have to pick up Axew from the Pokémon Center."

To wait to battle Axew, go to **PAGE 44**.

To continue on your journey, go to **PAGE 20**.

"Ossssshhhhaaaa," Oshawott says gently, releasing Water Gun.

Just like a hose, it fills the hole with water, creating the perfect swimming pool! So, you and your new Pokémon pal decide to take a break and splash around.

You joke, "I know you're cool, but I didn't think you'd help me cool off!"

"Osha, osha," it laughs.

Although you were nervous at first, it looks like you two have become fast friends.

THE END

I Choose You, Tepig!

You chose Tepig because you thought its feisty spirit would help in battle, but right now it's working against you in practice.

"Ember!" you command.

"Tepig!" it responds with a shot from its fiery nose—but it's headed straight at you!

"Ack!" you yell as you dodge the blast.

Clearly, it's time for a new plan.

If you want to take Tepig to the Pokémon Center to get some help from Nurse Joy, go to **PAGE 19**.

To leave Nuvema Town and just get started on your journey, go to **PAGE 32**.

You and Xian head to the Pokémon Center together. Along the way, Xian shows you the first Gym badge he earned in Unova: the Insect Badge.

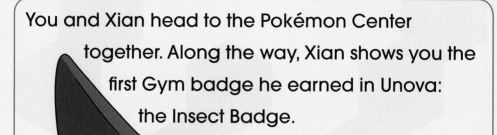

Xian says, "It was really fun to battle Burgh and his Bug-type Pokémon!"

If Xian has earned a Gym badge, you can probably learn a lot from his strategy. So, you and Snivy are extra excited as Axew and Xian arrive at the field, ready to battle.

To let Axew make the first move, proceed to **PAGE 62**.

To have Snivy start with Tackle, go to **PAGE 53**.

"Drillllllllbuuuuuuurrrrr!" the Ground-type shouts, as it jumps into the hole.

Oshawott stands on Drilbur's claws so Drilbur can lift Oshawott up high. You bend down and grab hold of Oshawott.

"Got ya!" you yell.

Now, Drilbur has to climb its way out of the hole too.

"Dri, dri, dri," it huffs and puffs.

Once Drilbur gets to the top, you give it a big thank you.

"Osha!" the Water-type says, hugging Drilbur.

Drilbur is happy to help, but now it's exhausted. Too bad; you would have really liked to battle it. Maybe another day… What's important is that you and Oshawott are back together again!

THE END

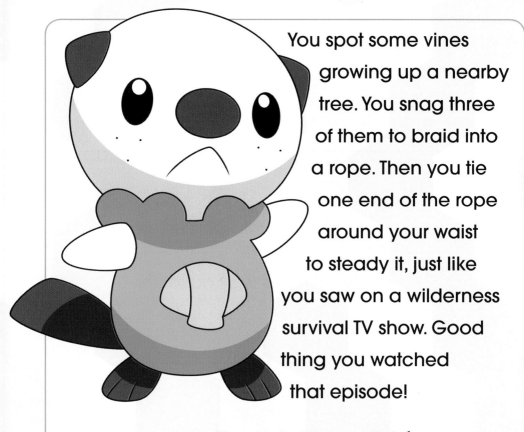

You spot some vines growing up a nearby tree. You snag three of them to braid into a rope. Then you tie one end of the rope around your waist to steady it, just like you saw on a wilderness survival TV show. Good thing you watched that episode!

You instruct your Pokémon friend, "Okay, Oshawott, grab onto the rope."

"Osha!" it responds.

You feel a tug, so you know it's ready to go. However, can it really climb its way out?

Continue to **PAGE 60**, **BOTTOM**.

Galvantula is dizzy from the swirling Leaf Tornado.

You tell Snivy, "Now, use Wrap on its legs."

Snivy ties up Galvantula.

"Awesome! Add Leech Seed to drain its power," you instruct.

Snivy's seeds stick to Galvantula, and its power is quickly sapped. It won't be bothering Minccino or Snivy anymore!

"Snivy!" the Grass-type says, lifting its head with pride.

Proceed to **PAGE 25**.

You carry Tepig, squealing and squirming, out the door of the Pokémon Center. With Tepig in your arms, now you can see the real problem—it has a prickly pebble stuck in its foot. No wonder it's been so upset!

"Don't worry, buddy. Hold still and I'll get it," you promise.

"Tepig!" it sighs with relief. All better!

"I'm sorry pal, I didn't realize you were hurting. From now on, just ask when you need help. That's what friends are for!" you say. Now, you are both ready to hit the road again.

You announce, "Adventure, here we come!"

"Tepig!" it cheers.

THE END

Minccino dodges your Poké Ball.

"Minccino!" it says, as it runs away.

You sigh, "Oh well, at least we tried!"

You thank Snivy for helping you rescue Minccino. One thing is for sure; you have a great friend in that Grass-type Pokémon—and one good pal is worth a million!

THE END

Snivy shoots Leech Seed.

"Minccinoooo!" it yells, dodging it.

Then, it runs off into the woods.

You shrug, "I guess that Pokémon wants to stay wild!"

No matter; you're proud that you and Snivy managed to rescue Minccino. Now it can roam free again.

THE END

Thanks to Defense Curl, Tepig is still in the game.

"Now, use Flame Charge!" you tell Tepig.

Swadloon blocks it with Protect and then goes for GrassWhistle.

"Swadlooooooooo," it sings.

Swadloon's song catches Tepig in a trance. Then, the Grass-type sinks its teeth into Tepig with Bug Bite and wins the match.

Like a good sport, you say, "Thanks for the battle."

Fitzy asks, "Would you like to join us for a post-game snack?"

If you would like some berries, go to **PAGE 61**.

If you just want to get back on the road, go to **PAGE 18**.

Minccino jumps in and gets Galvantula with Tickle.

"Gal, gal, gal!" Galvantula giggles.

Then, Snivy hits it with Tackle.

You tell it, "Snivy, add Wrap!"

Snivy squeezes the EleSpider Pokémon in its vines. Now, Galvantula is drained of its power. You win the battle!

"Way to go, Snivy and Minccino!" you cheer.

"Minccinoooooooo!" the Chinchilla Pokémon sighs, exhausted.

The poor Pokémon is pooped from such a crazy day! You decide to take your new pals to the Pokémon Center to get a good rest. They'll need it for the next adventure!

THE END

Snivy starts with Tackle. Axew dodges it and uses the close range to get Snivy with Scratch attack. Snivy responds with Wrap, but slippery Axew dodges that too.

"Axeeeeeeew!" it says, firing an incredible Dragon Rage.

Snivy gets zapped by Axew's big blast. After a long day, Snivy is too tired to keep battling. Axew wins the match. To show you're a good sport, you shake Xian's hand.

Xian compliments your teamwork, saying, "You and Snivy are an amazing team! I hope to get the chance to battle you both again."

"I'm looking forward to it!" you say.

THE END

While Tepig is in Defense Curl, Swadloon unleashes another String Shot to trap it.

Tepig responds by turning into a fast and furious Flame Charge fireball—"Teeeeepiiiiiig!"

However, Swadloon suddenly seems to be gaining energy. Bright white light surrounds it, and it evolves into Leavanny.

"Whoa!" you say, as your jaw drops.

"Leavanny!" it shouts, as it churns up a mighty Leaf Storm.

Tepig is caught in a green whirlwind. Leavanny wins the round.

Proud of Tepig's effort, you reassure it, "You were great, Tepig! I'm going to work hard at training so, someday, you'll be able to evolve too."

"Tepig!" it cheers.

THE END

"Tep tepig," it apologizes to Pansage.

You're happy to hear Tepig do the right thing and say it's sorry. Now you want to work with Tepig on your friendship. Nurse Joy offers to have Audino help the two of you have a heart-to-heart talk.

If you want to start off by telling Tepig that it's behaving badly, go to **PAGE 14**.

If you want to listen to what Tepig has to say first, go to **PAGE 28**.

With Galvantula out of the way, you toss a Poké Ball at Minccino.

However, can you really catch the Chinchilla Pokémon?

Continue to **PAGE 29**.

You quickly tell Snivy to use Leaf Tornado to scare off Galvantula. "Snivy!" it shouts, as it surrounds Galvantula with its Leaf Tornado attack.

Now you must decide whether to seize the moment and rescue Minccino, or keep pressing the battle with Galvantula.

If you think you can swoop in and save Minccino now, go to **PAGE 36**.

To keep battling Galvantula, go to **PAGE 47**.

Tepig shows Swadloon that it's sorry; it was an accident. Swadloon forgives Tepig.

"Tepig, I'm so proud of you for doing the right thing," you say.

Then, you suggest that you all have a battle to see if you can catch your new Pokémon friend. Swadloon nods.

"Tepig!" the Fire-type cheers.

It looks like the battle is on!

Proceed to **PAGE 40, TOP**.

You urge, "Snivy, don't let Minccino get away! Use Leaf Tornado."

Snivy has Minccino surrounded in swirling leaves. Now's your chance! You toss your Poké Ball.

Congratulations! You've caught your first new Pokémon pal.

"Hooray! I am so lucky to have two awesome new friends," you say.

"Snivy!" the Grass Snake Pokémon cheers.

THE END

Outside the Pokémon Center, Tepig is still using Ember.

"Tep tepig!" it snorts.

A Trainer with a tired Snivy comes up the path. You try to get Tepig to move out of their way, but that makes Tepig madder. It fires a big Ember fireball.

"Look out!" you warn.

However, Snivy cannot dodge it in time.

"Sniiiivy!" it sighs, falling over.

Continue to **PAGE 23**.

TOP

You and Oshawott make a break for it. Hiding behind some bushes, you can see Drilbur getting really angry about the state of its hole.

"Phew! That was a close one," you say with a sense of relief. "Osha!" it agrees.

The two of you decide to keep moving—you have many more adventures in store!

THE END

BOTTOM

"Osha, osha, osha!" it yelps, pulling itself up.

It looks like Oshawott can make it…unlike the rope. Just as Oshawott is about to reach the top, the vines snap apart. Oshawott falls back down the hole with a thud.

You ask your friend, "Oh no, are you okay?" "Oshaaaah," it sighs.

"Don't worry, buddy, I'll get you out of there!" you promise. It's time to go to plan B.

To wait for help, go to **PAGE 22**.

To have Oshawott try to use Water Gun to swim out, go to **PAGE 11**.

While you munch on berries under a shady tree, Fitzy tells you that he's impressed by how well you and Tepig worked together in your first battle.

"Thanks! But Tepig was being so testy before," you admit.

Fitzy points out that Tepig used that same fiery energy in a great way once it got the chance to use it on the battlefield.

"Wow, I didn't think of it that way!" you reply.

Fitzy adds, "You found a good friend when you picked Tepig."

"Yep, and now I've got a real pal named Fitzy too!" you say.

So, as you continue on your journey, you both hope to get the chance to battle again someday.

THE END

Axew tries to sneak up with Scratch attack, but Snivy surprises it with a green storm of Leaf Tornado. While Axew is surrounded, Snivy wraps it up with Vine Whip.

"Use Scratch attack to break out!" Xian shouts.

Before Axew has the chance, Snivy adds Leech Seed. Axew tries to dodge the power-draining seeds, but Snivy's aim is spot on. Axew's energy is completely sapped.

As a gracious competitor, Xian offers, "Congratulations on winning your first match!"

"Aw, shucks. Thank you so much for battling us," you reply. "You guys were awesome!"

"Snivy!" it agrees.

With a smile, Xian says, "Well, hopefully our paths will cross again."

"When they do, we'll be ready for a rematch!" you promise.

THE END

After all the trouble it caused, everyone is staring at Tepig, afraid of what it will do next.

"Tepiiiiiiig!" it cries, running out of the Pokémon Center, embarrassed.

You think to yourself, "Poor Tepig!" You run to catch up with your new Pokémon.

"Tepig, are you okay?" you ask.

Suddenly, Tepig realizes that it has a real friend. It nuzzles you because you stood by it, even through all of this. Now, your first Pokémon is a real pal to you too! You both decide to leave the Pokémon Center and start your adventure anew.

THE END

Glossary

arrive
to reach your destination

assure
to promise; to pledge

awesome
terrific; extraordinary;
inspiring awe

commotion
disturbance; noisy confusion;
excitement

compliment
praise; approve;
congratulate

confess
admit; own up; declare

counterattack
attack in response;
retaliate; revenge

diagonal
sloping; slanting

disappear
pass from view; vanish;
recede

distract
draw or direct attention
to a different object;
disturb; confuse

embarrassing
distressing; upsetting;
humiliating

encourage
inspire; support; persuade

evolve
change; advance;
develop; grow

exclaim
yell; shout; call out

exhausted
worn out; tired;
spent; depleted

express
communicate; say; explain

feisty
energetic; aggressive; lively

hoist
lift; raise; elevate

impress
strongly affect in thought or
feelings; influence in opinion

inspire
motivate; encourage;
stimulate

instruct
teach; command; tell

meantime
period in-between; interim;
time being

nuzzle
snuggle; burrow or root up
with the nose or snout

photosynthesis
the forming of complex
materials with the aid of
light as an energy source

prey
victim; target

proceed
continue; advance; carry on

reasoning
thinking; logic; forming
conclusions or judgments
from facts

respect
sense of worth; admiration;
high opinion

sapped
weakened; exhausted;
tired; worn out

seize
grab; capture;
take control of

signal
indicate; announce;
mark; communicate

snarl
growl; roar; sneer

spunk
toughness; spirit;
courage; boldness

suggest
recommend; propose; advise

survival
the continuation of life
or existence

testy
grumpy; impatient; cranky;
bad-tempered

unleash
release; let loose; set free

wilderness
a wild, uninhabited, or
uncultivated area